I0113752

An aubergine automobile accelerated audaciously along Acacia Avenue almost accomplishing an awful and apocalyptic accident and antagonising an aged, articulate, altruistic and agrestically awkward American astronaut, an air-headed, armour-plated armadillo and an artistically audacious aardvark.

F

P

M

S

" Travelling — it leaves you speechless
then turns you into a storyteller.

Ibn Battuta

A 100-Word Mystery

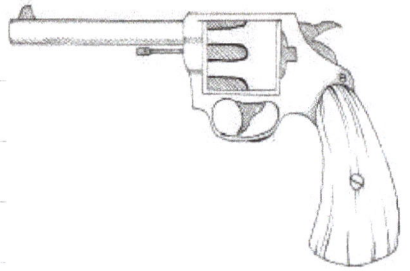

" A writer is a world trapped in a person.

Victor Hugo

How to stop time: *kiss.*

How to travel in time: *read.*

How to escape time: *music.*

How to feel time: *write.*

How to release time: *breathe.*

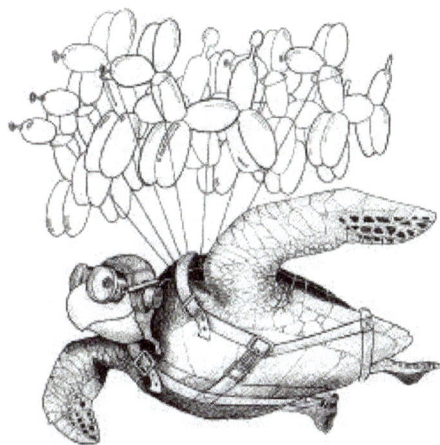

" Sometimes I think we're alone in the universe,
and sometimes I think we're not.
In either case the idea is quite staggering.

Arthur C. Clarke

Rapunzel & Hercule Poirot

in a Gondola

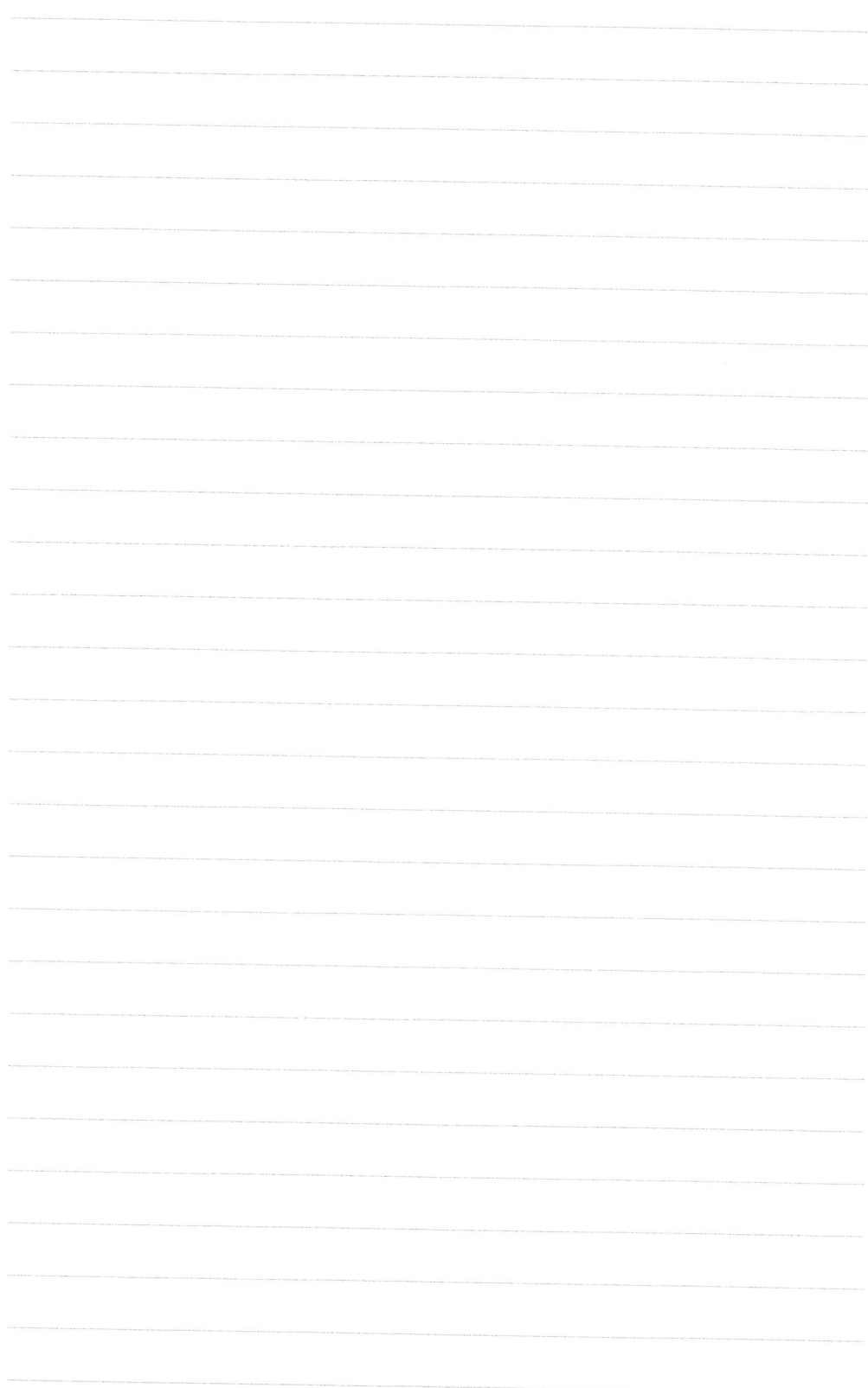

" The world is full of magic things, patiently waiting
for our senses to grow sharper.

William Butler Yeats

Six one-page scene builders.

Write six versions of your walk through a fairground.

Take the same route each time; but with each version,
layer in different aspects.

You only have one page for each walk,
so you will need to adapt or drop some things
to fit the new senses into subsequent descriptions.

On your first walk through, write only
what you can see – with no colours, smells or sounds.

Rewrite that same scene adding in the colours.

Rewrite the scene again, layering it with sounds.

Rewrite again, this time weaving in the smells.

And again, adding in anything you might touch.

Finally, rewrite your route through the fairground incorporating
as many of the sights, colours sounds and textures
you used previously – but this time
write the sense-filled scene as if you are being pursued,
or you are chasing someone.

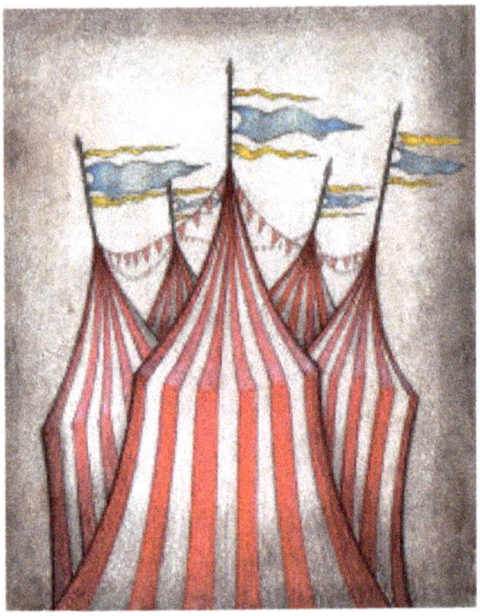

"Imagination is the only weapon in the war against reality.

Lewis Carroll, *Alice in Wonderland*

CINQUAIN

FIRST LINE:
Noun

SECOND LINE:
2 adjectives

THIRD LINE:
3 'ing' words

FOURTH LINE:
4-word description

FIFTH LINE:
Synonym
for first line

Winter

Acrobat

Fearless, masterful

Leaping, swinging, balancing

Walks on a trapeze

Daredevil

Violin

> "We're our own dragons as well as our own heroes,
> and we have to rescue ourselves from ourselves.
>
> Tom Robbins

X Treasure!

Loot!

N (compass)

Sharks

- - - 3 steps

Snakes

Monster!

Forest

Death

Mountains

" An idea that is not dangerous
is unworthy of being called an idea at all.

Oscar Wilde

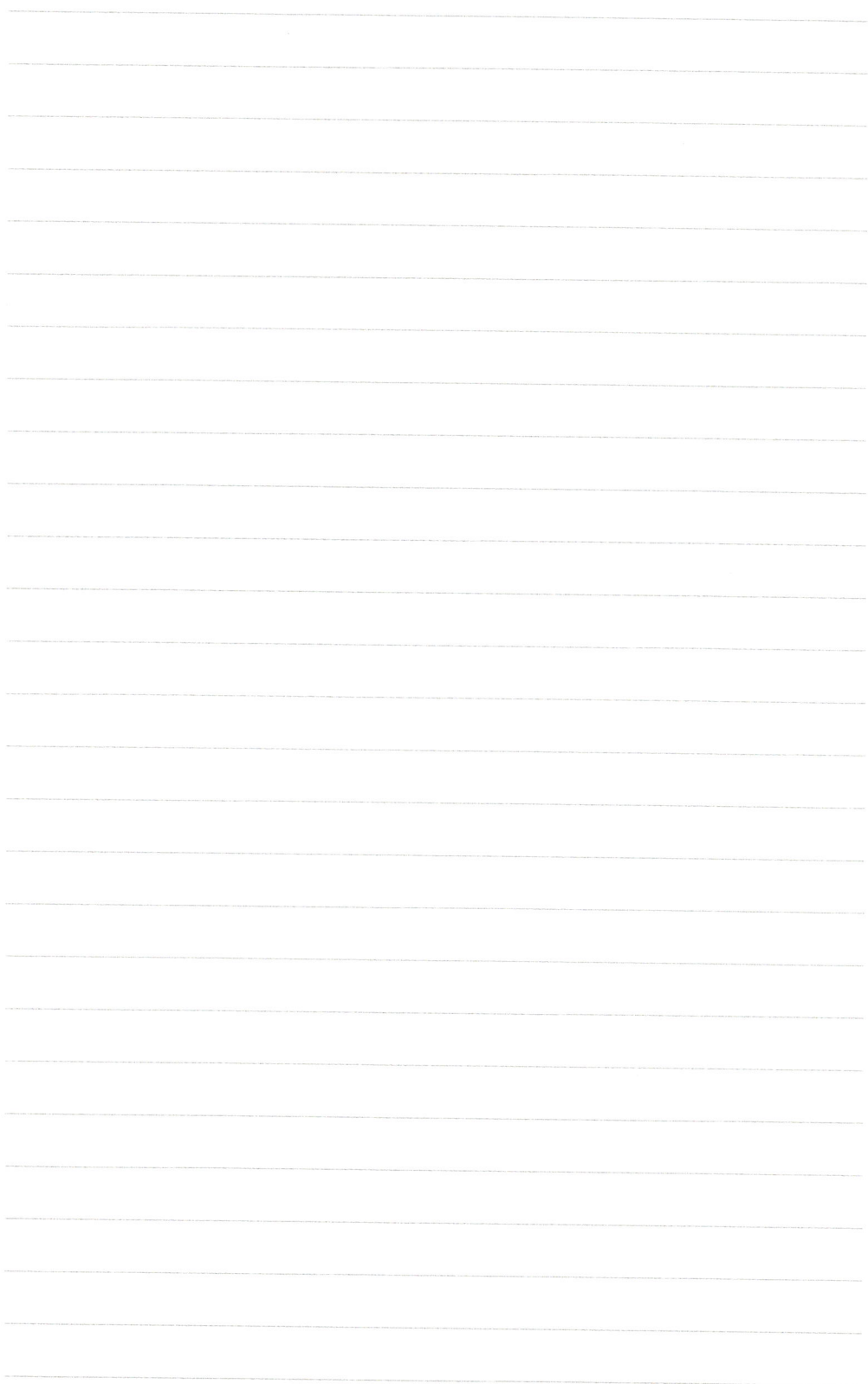

"You become responsible, forever, for what you have tamed.

Antoine de Saint-Exupery

EVERMORE

“Fairy tales are more than true: not because
they tell us that dragons exist,
but because they tell us dragons can be beaten.

Neil Gaimain, *Coraline*

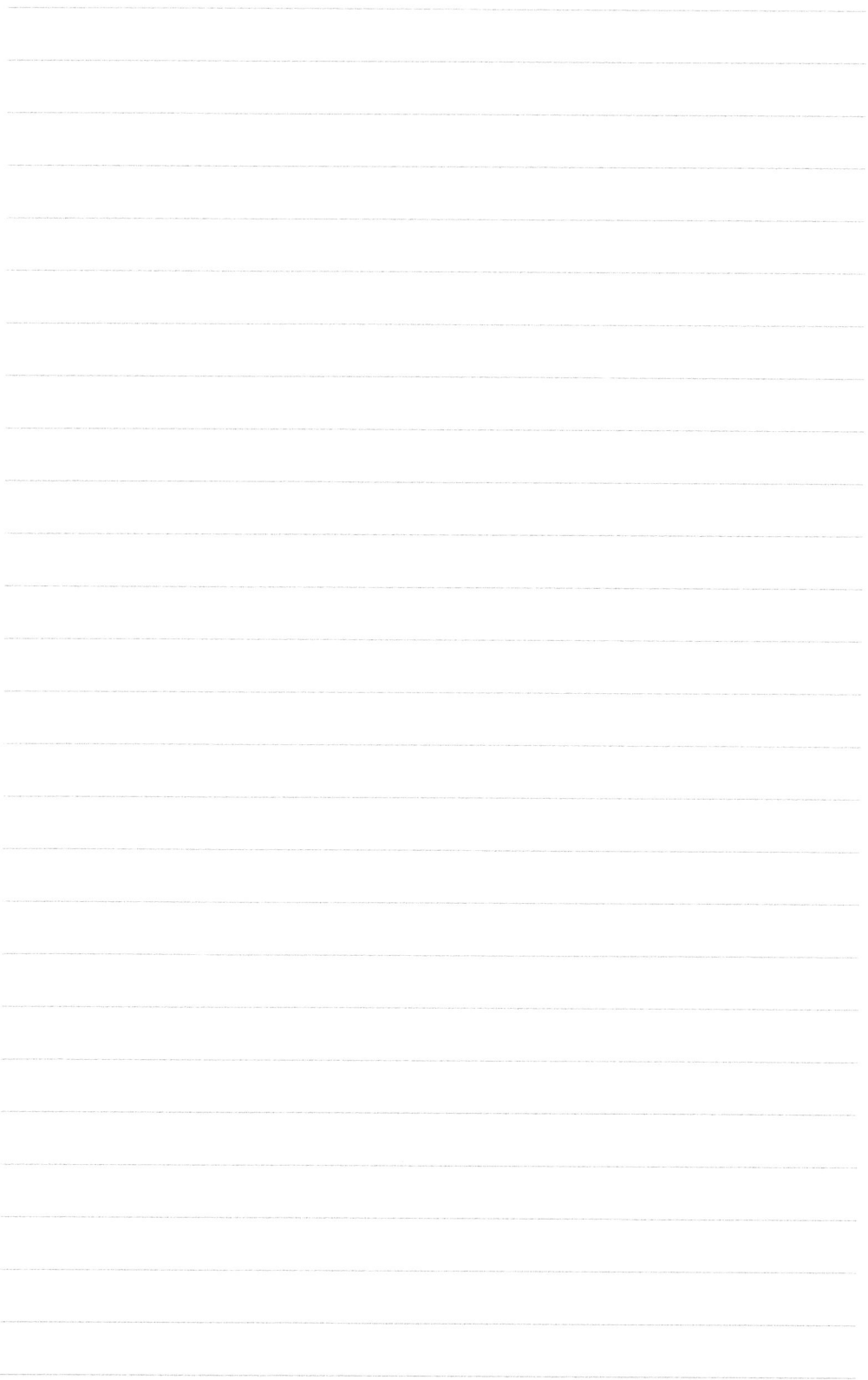

"To create one's world in any of the arts takes courage.

Georgia O'Keefe

"My imagination makes me human and makes me a fool;
it gives me all the world and exiles me from it.

Ursula K. Le Guin

" Learn the rules like a pro,
    so you can break them like an artist.
                    Pablo Picasso

"Flying is learning how to throw yourself at the ground and miss.

Douglas Adams

"Logic will get you from A to Z.
Imagination will get you everywhere.
Albert Einstein

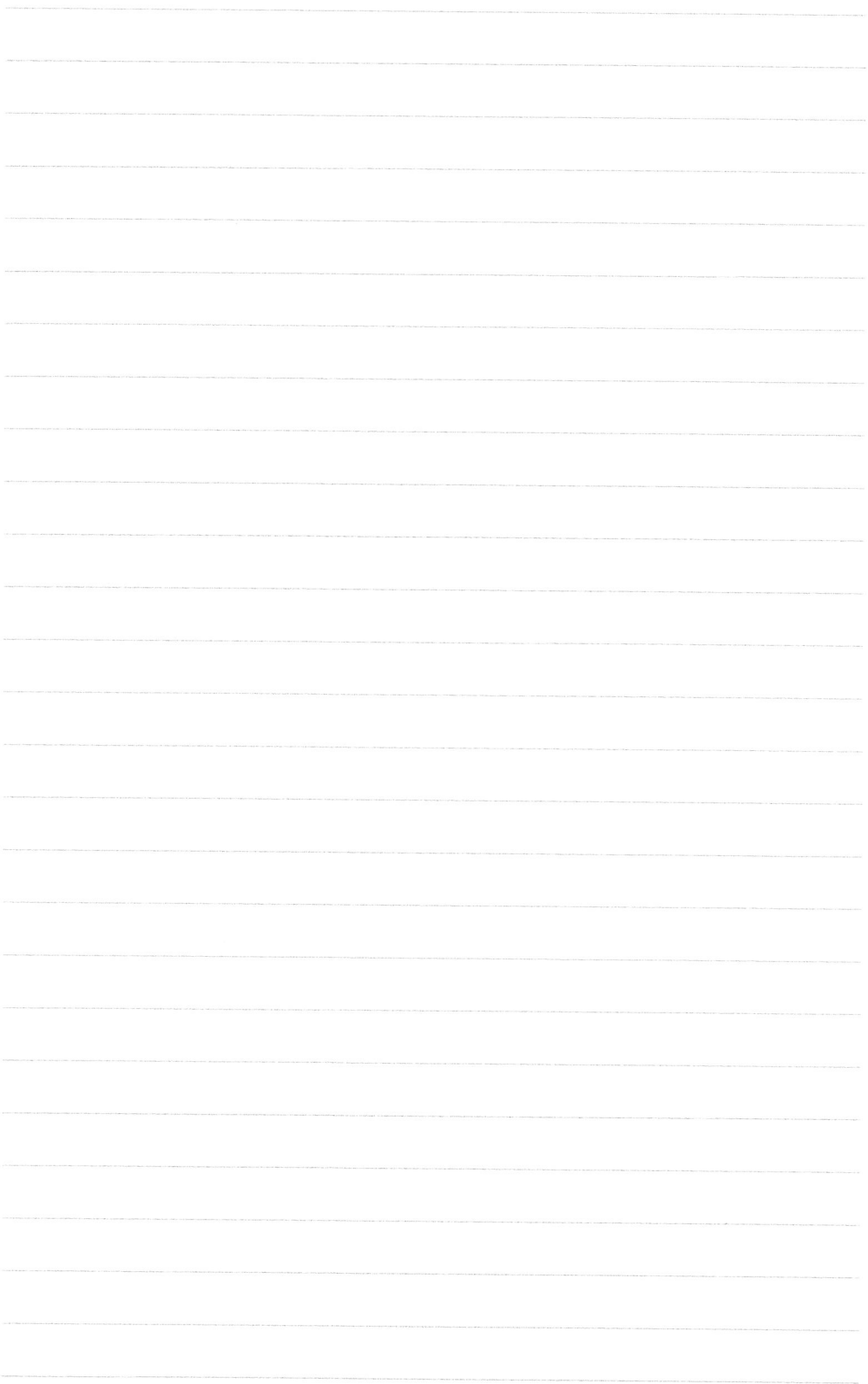

"To be an artist means never to avert one's eyes.

Akira Kurosawa

"Music expresses that which cannot be put into words and that which cannot remain silent.

Victor Hugo

"Description begins in the writer's imagination,
but should finish in the reader's.

Stephen King

" Where there is no imagination there is no horror.

Arthur Conan Doyle

63

"Invention, it must be humbly admitted, does not consist
in creating out of void but out of chaos.

Mary Shelley, *Frankenstein*

俳句

Three lines

17 syllables

Whisper overhead
A wanderer of the sea
On its lonely flight

First line – 5 syllables

Second line – 7 syllables

Third line – 5 syllables

" To realise the unimportance of time is the gate to wisdom.

Bertrand Russell

Time of your life

Time flies

For the time being

It's high time

What's the time, Mr Wolf?

Time will tell

Time travel

Time warp

Tea time

It's time

A stich in time

Wibbly-wobbly timey-wimey stuff

Killing time

Time is of the essence

Time out

Time heals all wounds

As time goes by

Behind the times

A waste of time

Ozymandias

Percy Bysshe Shelley

I met a traveller from an antique land
Who said: 'Two vast and trunkless legs of stone
Stand in the desert. Near them, on the sand,
Half sunk, a shattered visage lies, whose frown,
And wrinkled lip, and sneer of cold command,
Tell that its sculptor well those passions read
Which yet survive, stamped on these lifeless things,
The hand that mocked them and the heart that fed:
And on the pedestal these words appear:
"My name is Ozymandias, king of kings:
Look on my works, ye Mighty, and despair!"
Nothing beside remains. Round the decay
Of that colossal wreck, boundless and bare
The lone and level sands stretch far away.'

Ozymandias

Horace Smith

In Egypt's sandy silence, all alone,
Stands a gigantic Leg, which far off throws
The only shadow that the Desert knows.
'I am great Ozymandius,' saith the stone,
'The King of Kings; this mighty City shows
'The wonders of my hand." The City's gone!
Nought but the Leg remaining to disclose
The site of this forgotten Babylon.
We wonder, and some Hunter may express
Wonder like ours, when thro' the wilderness
Where London stood, holding the wolf in chase,
He meets some fragment huge, and stops to guess
What powerful but unrecorded race
Once dwelt in that annihilated place.

In 1818 two English poets were challenged to write poems inspired by the British Museum's recent archaeological acquisition from Egypt: huge stone fragments of a mighty statue of Pharaoh Ramses II. While both explored notions of fate and the ravages of time, Shelley looked back on the lost world of the pharaohs while Smith warned that even 'modern' London might one day be nothing. Shelley's sonnet was first published in *The Examiner* in London, on January 11, 1818. Smith's first appeared in *The Examiner* a few weeks later. 'Ozymandias' was the Greek name for the Pharaoh Ramses II.

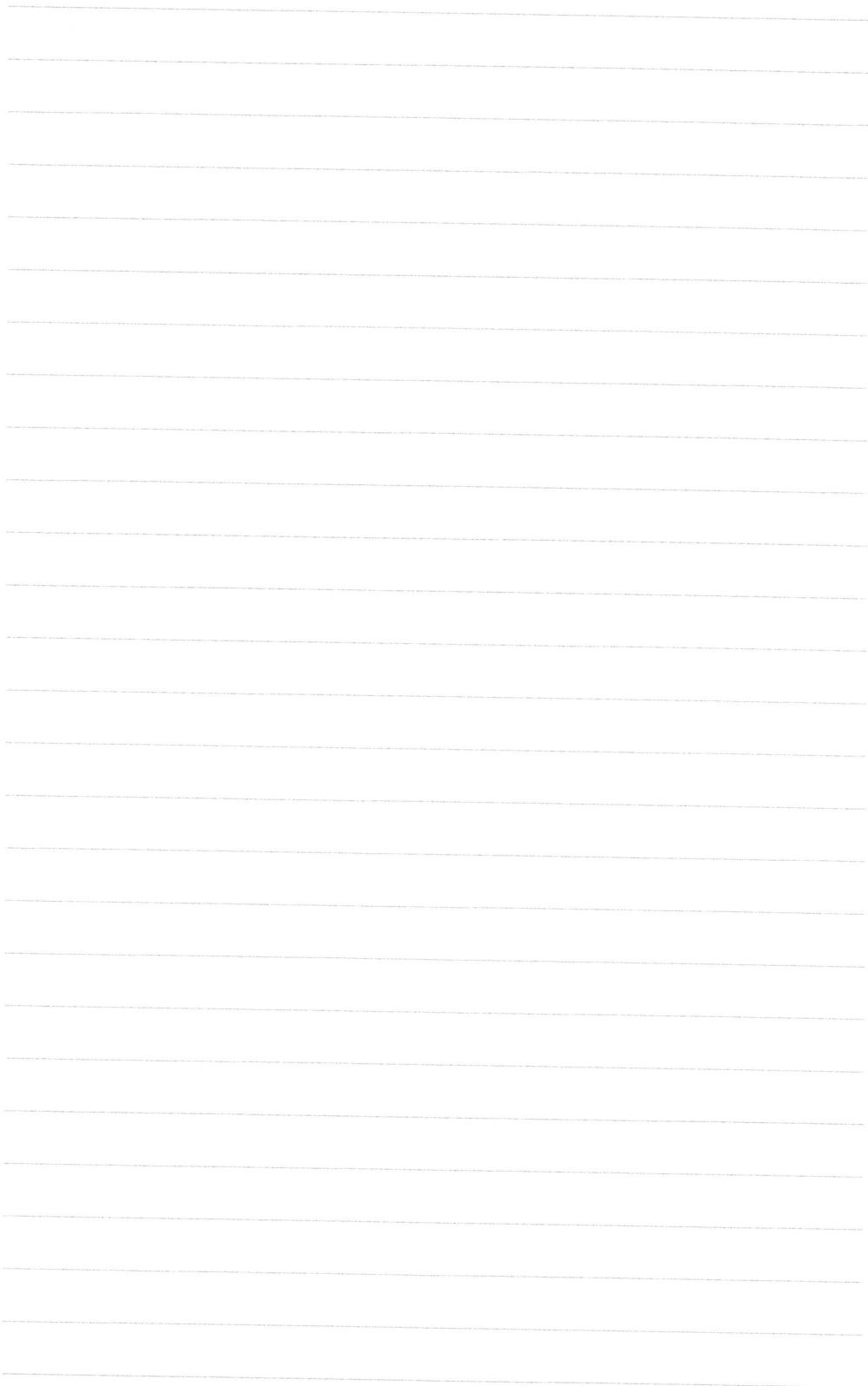

It   a

that   in

be   a   .

takes   to   there

and   .

of   the   , the   ,

the   , the   .

It   a

that   in

be   a

      .

To

That

a   .

They   a   of

before   of

overtakes

of   and   .

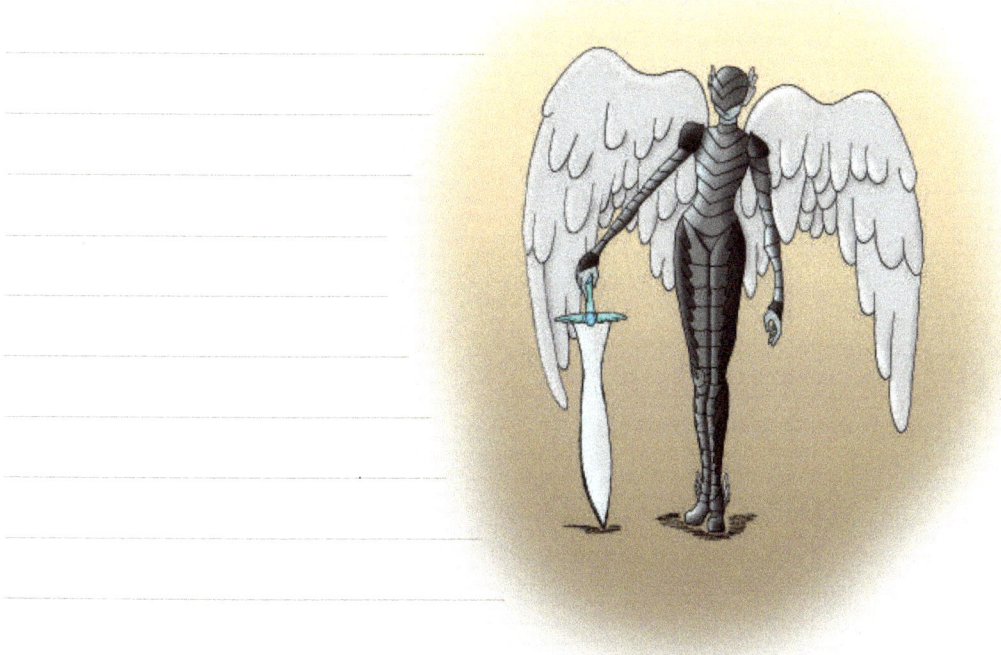

" You see things; and you say, 'why?'
    But I dream things that never were; and I say, 'Why not?'

George Bernard Shaw

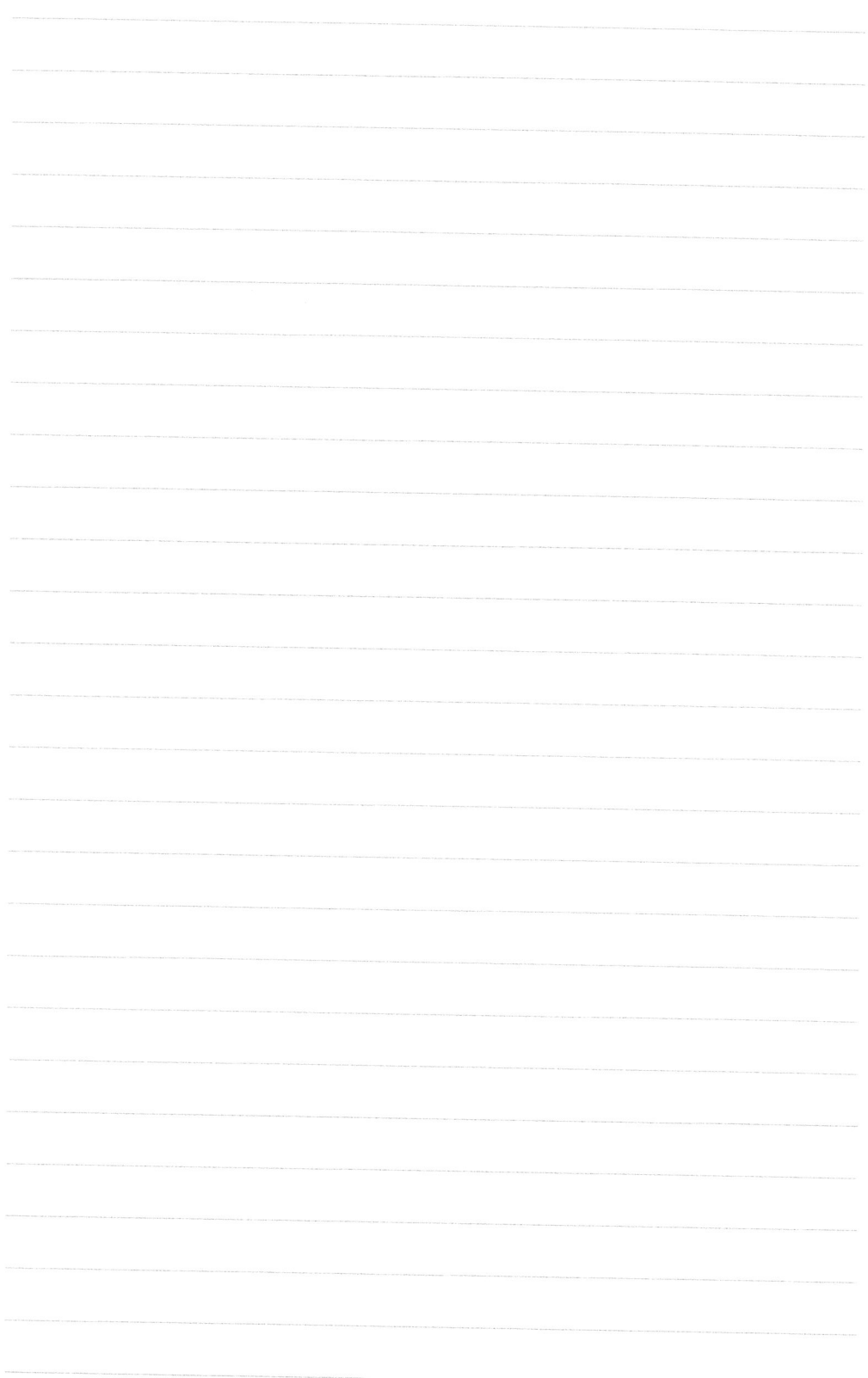

> *Someone to tell it to, is one*
> *of the fundamental needs of human beings.*
>
> Miles Franklin

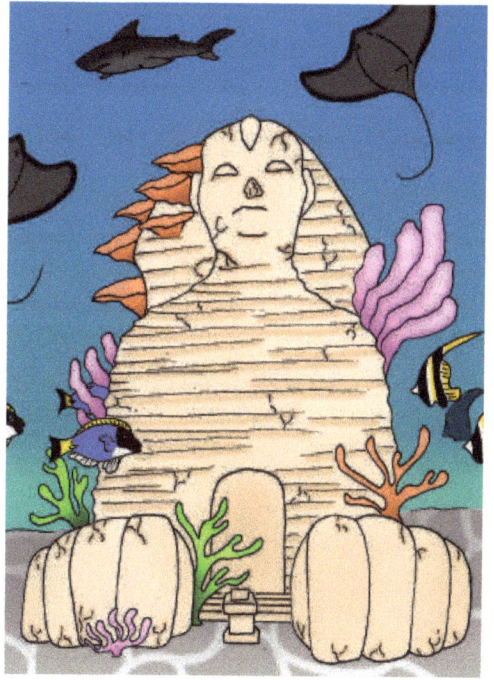

CIRCUMVENT THE CLICHÉ

Avoid clichés like the plague

A knight in shining tinfoil

If you can't beat them, whip them into a frenzy

Time flies when you throw a clock

The best things in life are really expensive

Too many cooks spoil the diet

Waiting with baited fish hook

What goes around comes up behind you

The grass is always greener where the cow pats are

A rose by any other name could be a daffodil

To be or not to be that is a cliché

What comes out?

> "Normal is not something to aspire to,
> it's something to get away from.
>
> Jodie Foster

A MAP BEGINS THE QUEST

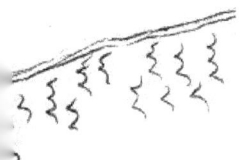

> **"** Scheherazade is one of the great authorless figures.
> No one has any idea who made her up,
> so it's easy to think she made herself up.
>
> Salman Rushdie

Without Shakespeare

these words would not exist

pre-meditated
assassination
fairyland
besmirch
SWAGGER
RADIANCE
CIRCUMSTANTIAL
Cold-blooded
Moonbeam
Zany
Laughing Stock
Green-eyed
BAITED
OBSCENE
grovel
BREATH
puking
Gloomy
DISCONTENT
lacklustre
mealy-mouthed
VILLAINOUS

Before *Infinite Possibility*

these words did not exist

triantiwat
qwarding
OOFRAP
verlon
EE-WA
NAART
pultard
intresiac
AFFERDOOL
Ferland
JERBANUM
SELLUND
TITTERYNOB

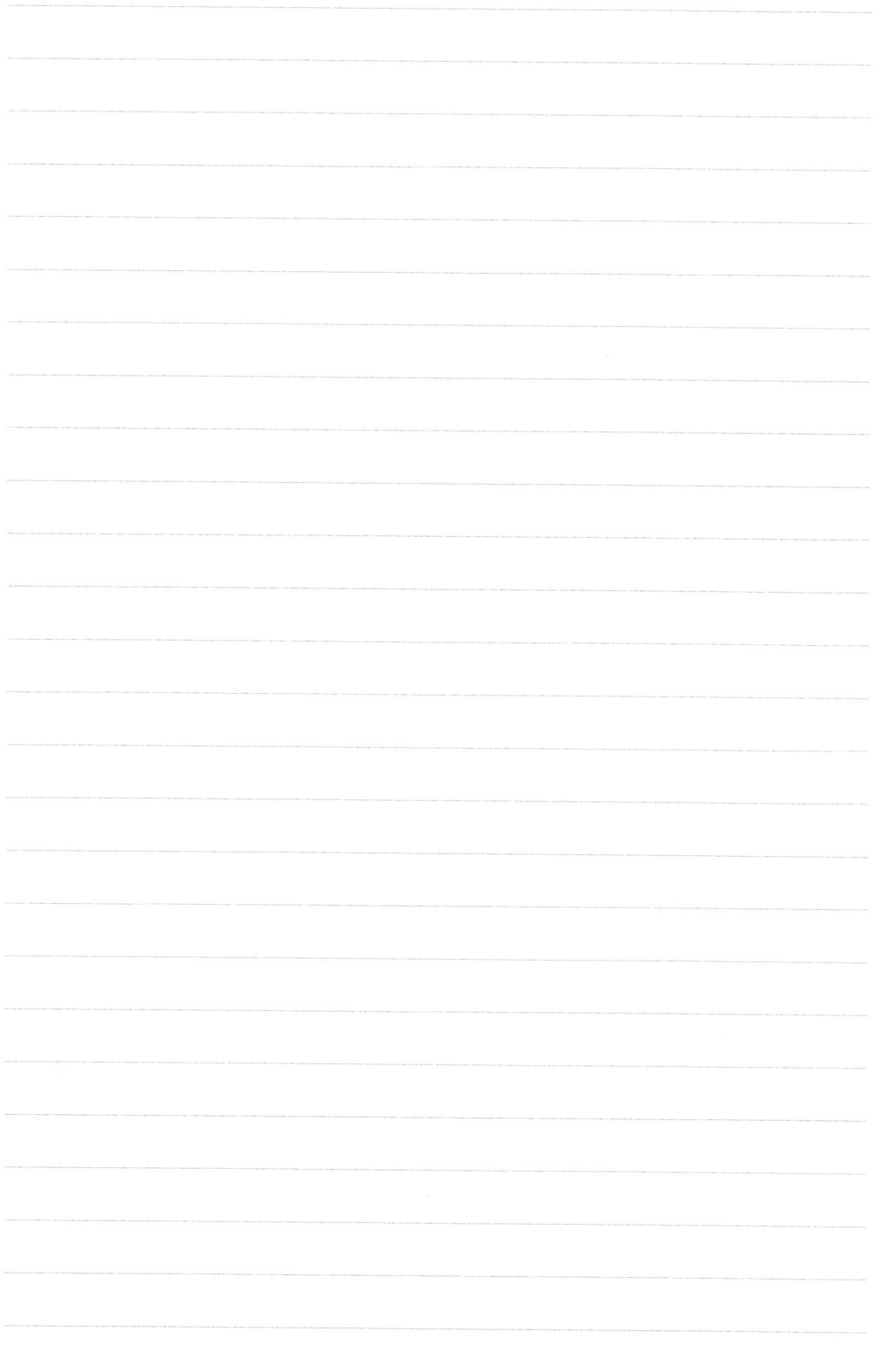

ALPHABETITIS

A beautiful cat did everything ferociously: grooming, hunting, intimidating jaguar kittens, licking moth-eaten, naughty old pussy-quills, ravishing studious tigers under vociferously wandering xenophobic yawning zebras.

Red

Blue

"Once you eliminate the impossible, whatever remains,
no matter how improbable, must be the truth.

Arthur Conan Doyle

SESTINA

A sestina is a fixed verse poem consisting of six stanzas, each of six lines, followed by a three-line tercet (aka an *envoi*).

The words that end each line rotate in a set pattern (as numbered); with the last word of each verse becoming the last word of the first line of the next verse.

Each line of a sestina can be simple or complex, in terms of the number of words.

Try these prompt words; and then choose six of your own.

1 _____ earth

2 _____ silver

3 _____ fall

4 _____ laughing

5 _____ lies

6 _____ calm

6 _____ calm

1 _____ earth

5 _____ lies

2 _____ silver

4 _____ laughing

3 _____ fall

3 _____ fall

6 _____ calm

4 _____ laughing

1 _____ earth

2 _____ silver

5 _____ lies

5	....	lies
3	....	fall
2	....	silver
6	....	calm
1	....	earth
4	....	laughing

4	....	laughing
5	....	lies
1	....	earth
3	....	fall
6	....	calm
2	....	silver

2	....	silver
4	....	laughing
6	....	calm
5	....	lies
3	....	fall
1	....	earth

2,5	....	silver	....	lies
4,3	....	laughing	....	fall
6,1	....	calm	....	earth

The stength of the sestina is the repetition and recycling of elusive patterns that cannot be quite held in the mind all at once.

Stephen Fry

A 100-Word Fairytale

"Don't you love the Oxford Dictionary? When I first read it, I thought it was a really really long poem about everything.

David Bowie

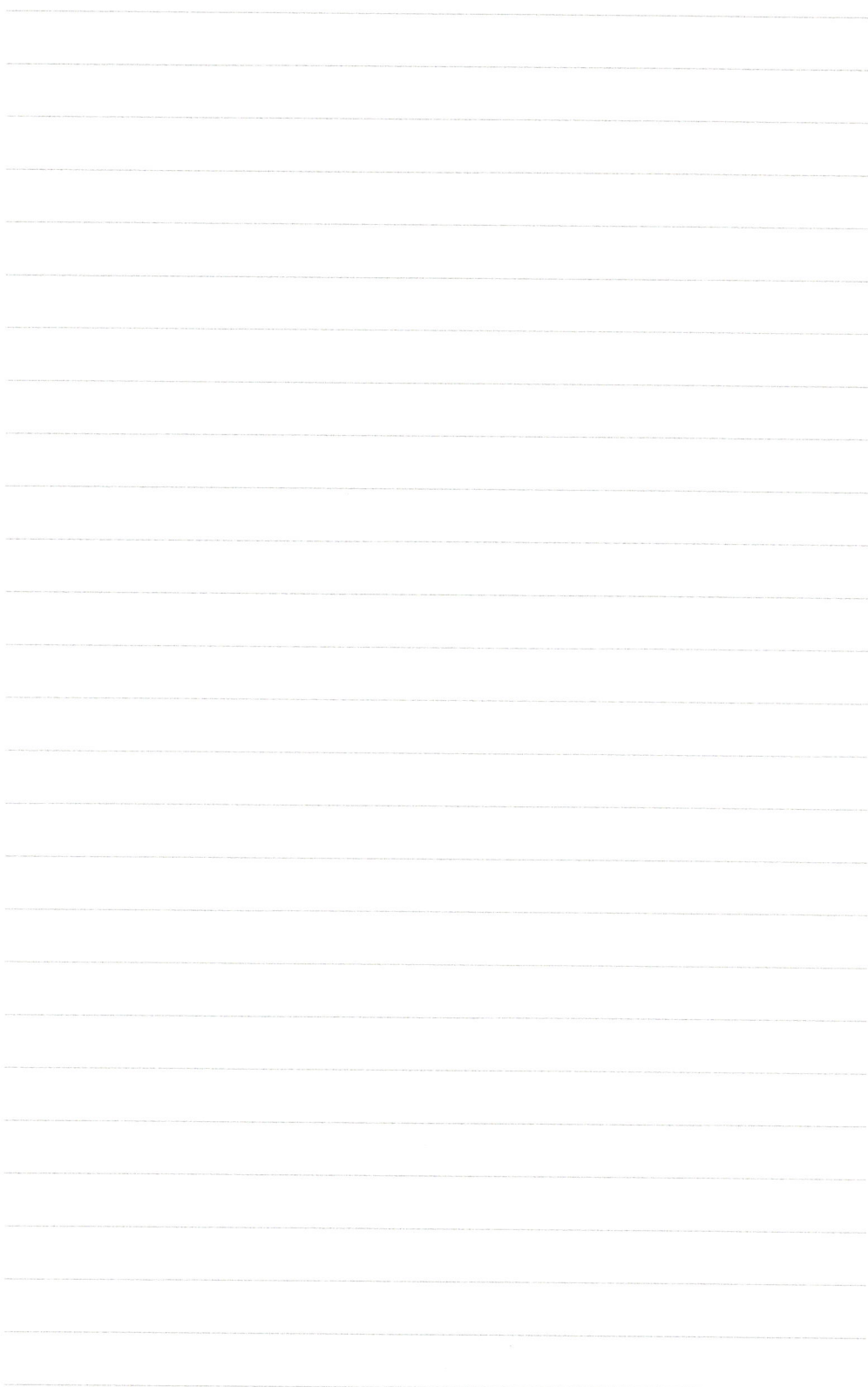

Cleopatra & Eliza Dolittle
at a car rally

Cathy Freeman &
Xena Warrior Princess
in a space shuttle

Galileo & Furiosa
on Easter Island

Atticus Finch &
Alexander the Great
in a submarine

Freddie Mercury &
Phryne Fisher
on a bullet train

THE BUTTERFLY EFFECT

A hypothetical example of *chaos theory* which illustrates how any small action may cause huge unforseen consequences.

The fluttering of a butterfly's wings on the steppes of Mongolia might cause a cyclone on the the island of Mauritius.

" The most difficult thing is the decision to act,
the rest is merely tenacity.

Amelia Earhart

To Boldly Split the Infinitive

or, Frankly My Dear, Not to Give a Damn

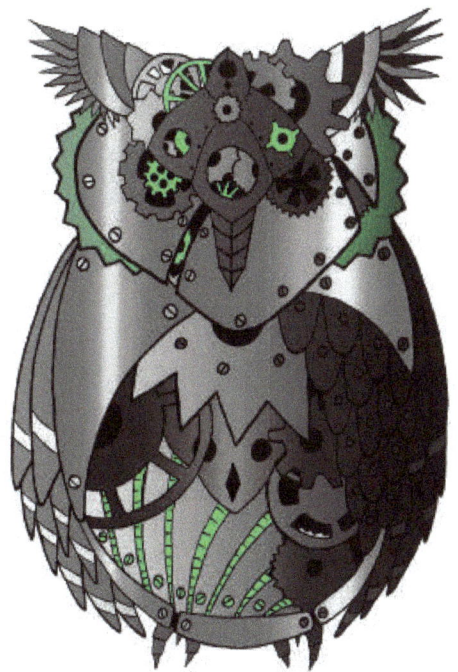

A VIRULENT VIRUS

A Global Pandemic of...
A Sudden Disappearance of...

GREED

MEN

IMAGINATION

FOSSIL FUELS

FEAR

BIRDS

COMPASSION

CATS

GOLD

WOMEN

LOVE

POETRY

AGEING

MONEY

GOATS

ANTS

RELIGION

ANGER

GERMS

FISH

BEES

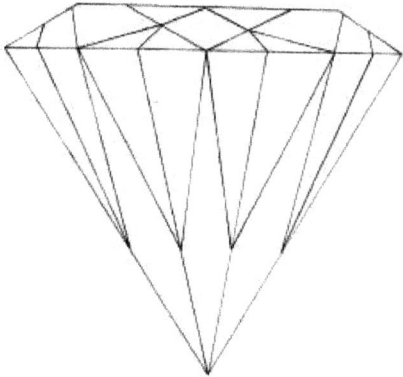

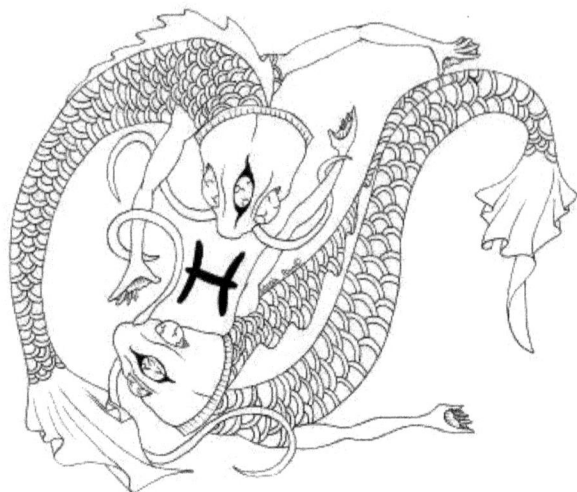

" If you want your children to be intelligent, read them fairy tales.
If you want them to be more intelligent, read them more fairy tales.
                                                    Albert Einstein

> **"**We read to know that we are not alone.

William Nicholson

> "Why do the men come, do you suppose?

> "Who knows why men do anything?

Richard Adams, *Watership Down*

"I don't pretend we have all the answers but the questions are certainly worth thinking about.

Arthur C. Clarke

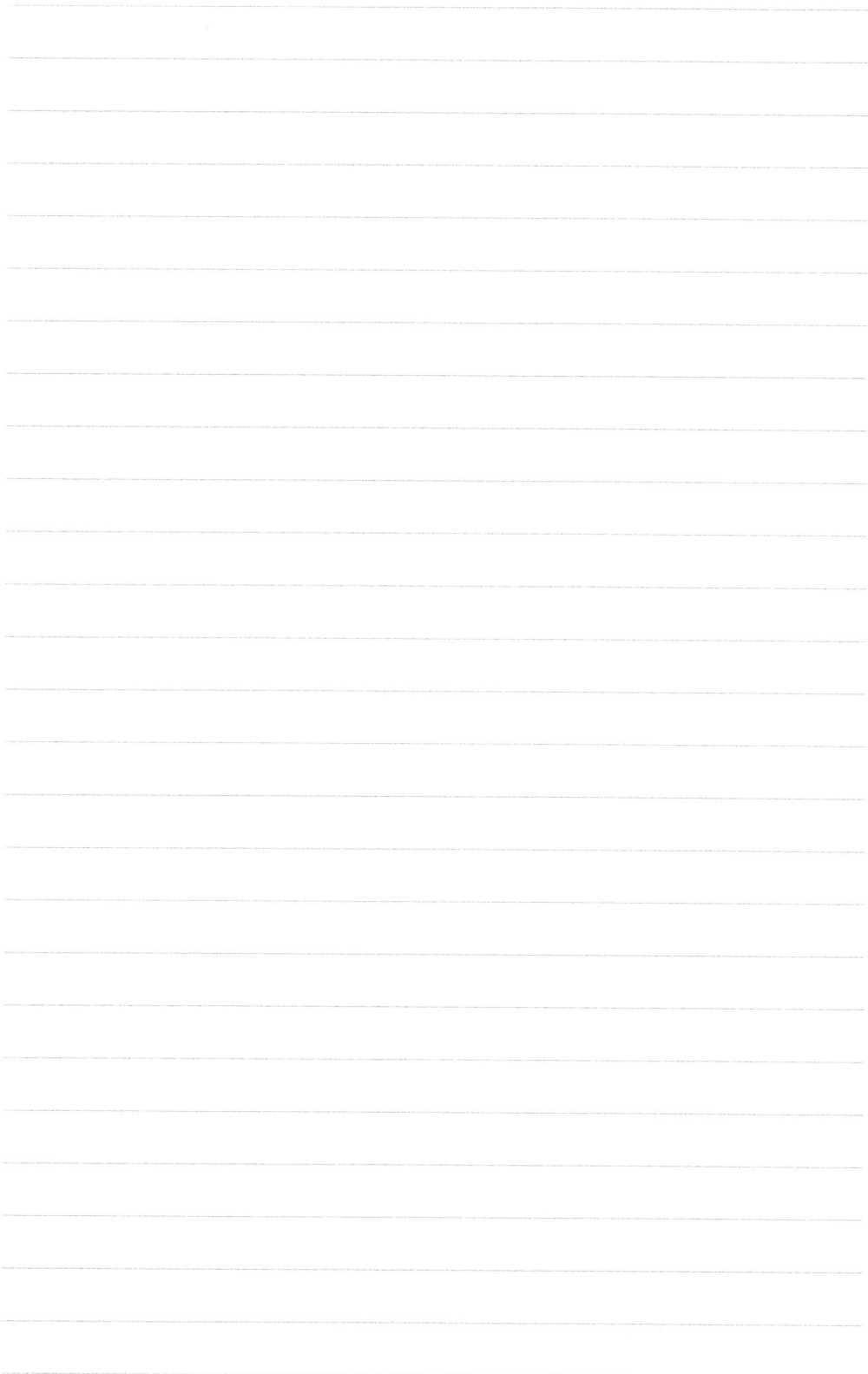

> "Endless forms most beautiful and most wonderful have been, are being, evolved.

Charles Darwin

"The thing under my bed waiting to grab my ankle isn't real.
I know that, and I also know that if I'm careful to keep
my foot under the covers, it will never be able to grab my ankle.

Stephen King

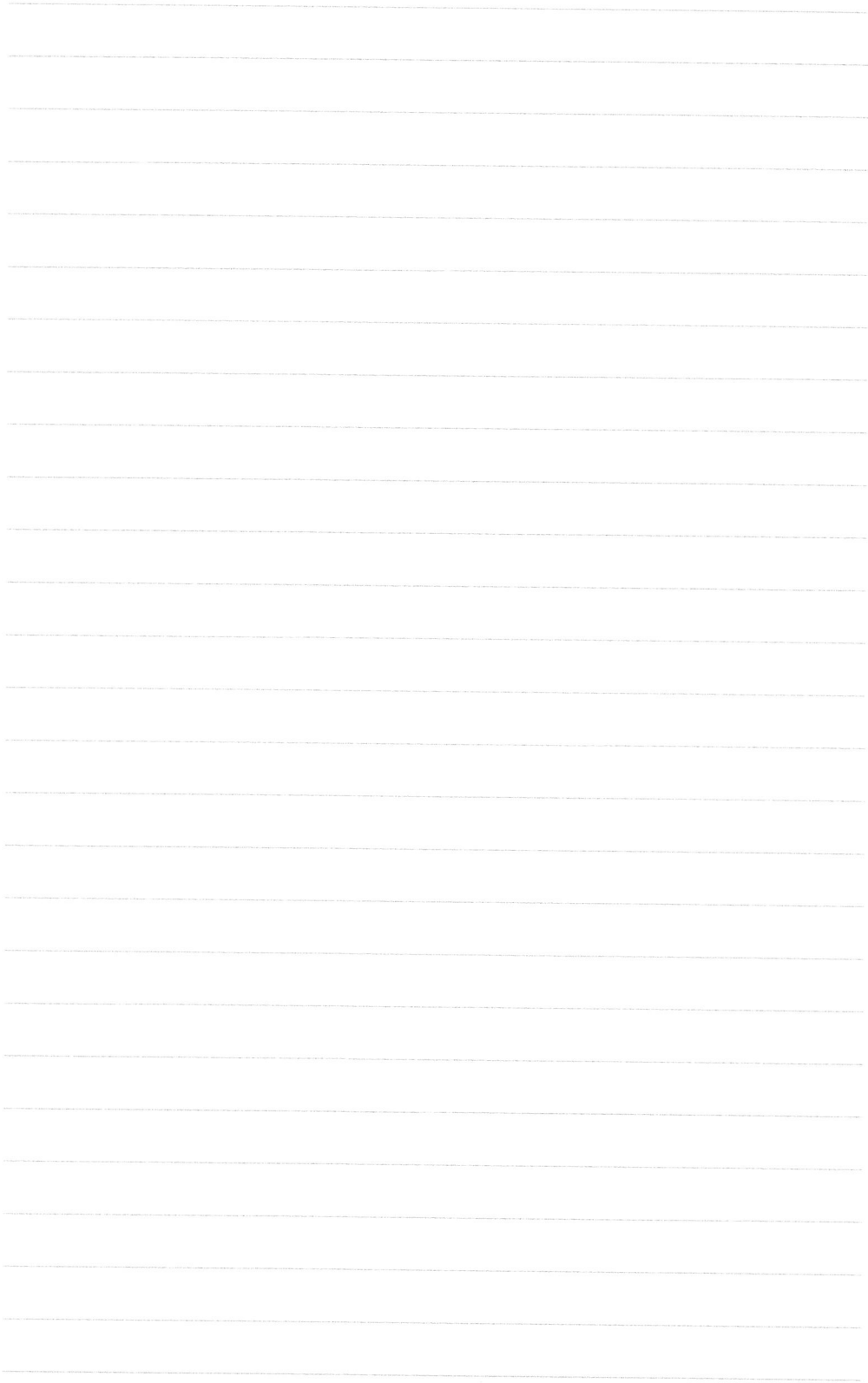

"There is a theory which states that if ever anyone discovers what the Universe is for, it will instantly disappear and be replaced by something even more bizarre and inexplicable.
There is another theory which states that this has already happened.

Douglas Adams

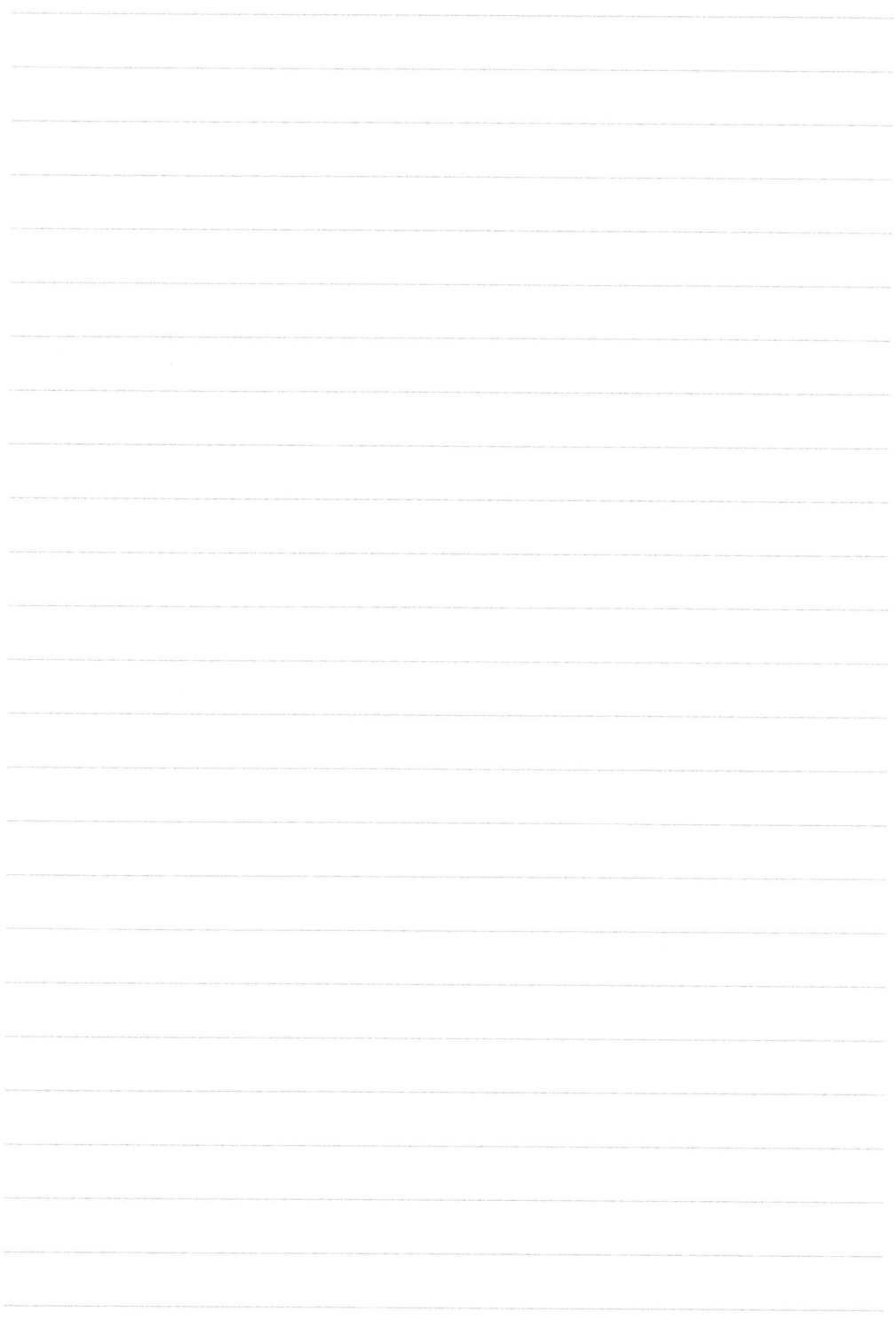

"Beware of monotony;
it's the mother of all the deadly sins.

Edith Wharton

"*Any sufficiently advanced technology
is indistinguishable from magic.*

Arthur C Clarke

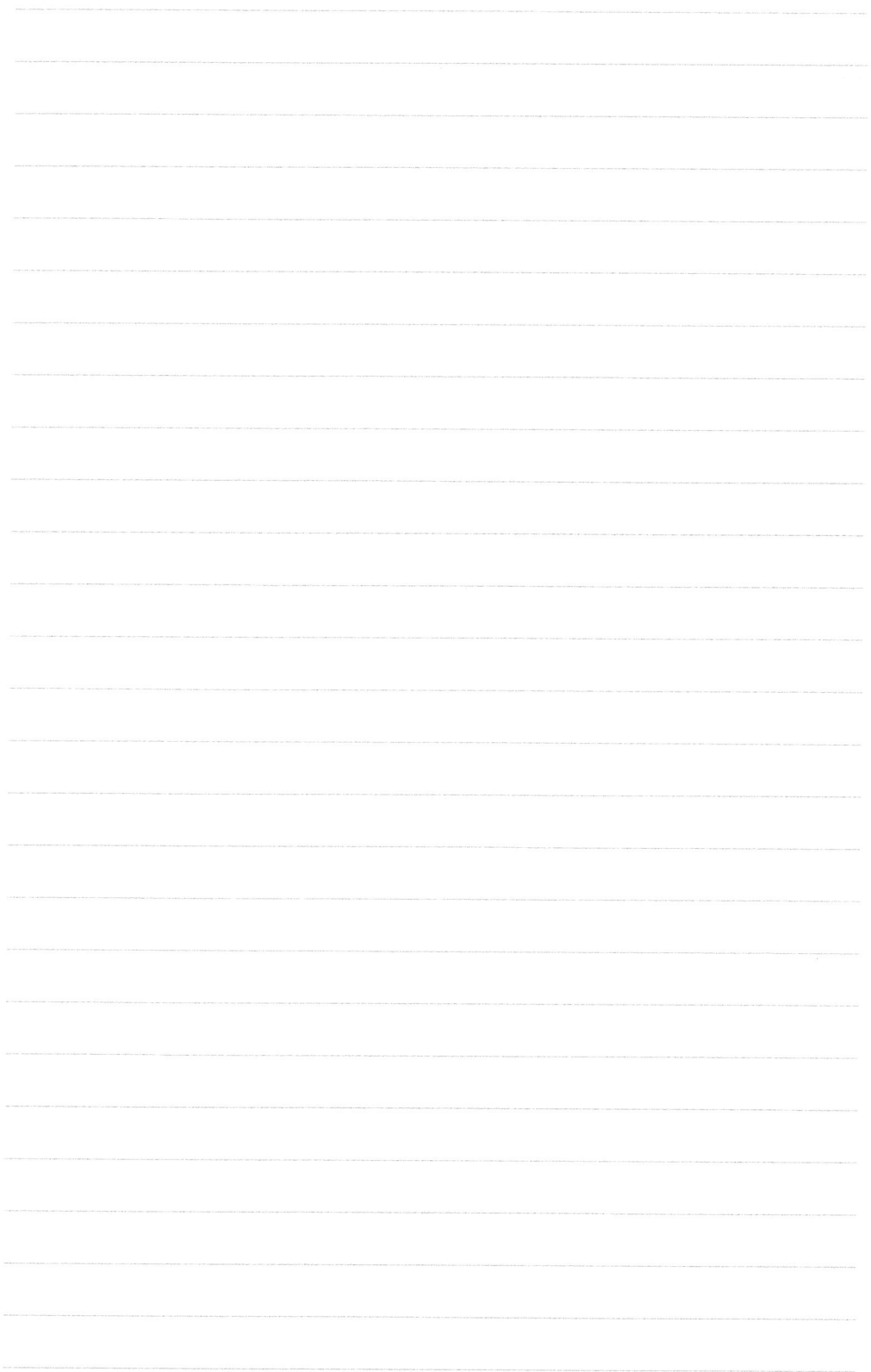

This edition published in Australia inn 2020
by Clan Destine Press
PO Box 121 Bittern
Victoria 3918 Australia

Copyright © Lindy Cameron / Clan Destine Press 2016

First published as *The Journal of Infinite Possibility* in Australia 2016

All rights reserved. No part of this book may be reproduced or transmitted in any form
or by any means, including internet search engines and retailers, electronic or mechanical,
photocopying (except under the statutory exceptions provisions of the *Australian Copyright Act* 1968),
recording or by any information storage and retrieval system,
without prior permission in writing from the publisher.

National Library of Australia Cataloguing-in-Publication entry
Author: Cameron, Lindy
Title: *Never Bored*

ISBN: 978-0-6487414-9-7

Clan Destine
P R E S S

Cover crow: Sarah Pain
Cover illustration: Ashlea Bechaz
Cover design: Willsin Rowe

Internal illustrations & photos:-

Sarah Pain: 1, 8, 10, 16, 32, 33, 39, 40, 47, 51, 52, 56, 58, 60, 68, 70, 73,
75, 76, 79, 82, 86, 112, 115, 117, 120, 126, 129, 130, 139.

from CDP's *Colouring Horrorscope* by Sarah Pain: 60 & 120

Ashlea Bechaz: 2, 7, 27, 42, 54, 55, 64, 89, 93, 94, 102, 108, 123, 132, 136.
from CDP's *Colouring Bazaar* by Ashlea Bechaz: 2, 89, 132.
from CDP's *A.K.A. Fudgepuddle* by Fin J Ross: 27, 54, 55, 93, 102.

Vicky Pratt: 13, 19, 20, 30, 31, 35, 44, 48, 63, 80, 85, 100, 107, 110, 118.
from CDP's *And Then... the Great Big Book of Awesome Adventure Tales*, various authors: 63 & 85.

Loraine Cooper: 22 & 36, 135.

Ran Valerhon: 124 & 125
from CDP's *Arrabella Candellarbra & the Questy Thing to End All Questy Things* by A.K. Wrox: 124 & 125.

Design & Typesetting: Clan Destine Press
Printed and bound in Australia by Lightning Source

www.ingramcontent.com/pod-product-compliance
Lightning Source LLC
Chambersburg PA
CBHW051435270326
41935CB00019B/1836